# Glimpsing the DIVINE
## THE JESSE TREE DEVOTIONALS

**Blake A. Hiemstra**     **Illustrated by Andrea Van Wyk Kamper**

*Andrea Van Wyk Kamper*

CREATE SPACE

*Glimpsing the Divine*
Copyright © 2012 by Blake A. Hiemstra & Andrea Van Wyk Kamper

ISBN-13: 978-1478339335

*Cover design: Kara Ledeboer*
*Cover artwork and all interior artwork: Andrea Van Wyk Kamper*
*Author photograph: Carla Hiemstra*
*Illustrator photograph: Third Element Studios*

*Printed in the United States of America*

*For C, my soul mate, and Team Hiemstra, one special crew.*

*To George G. Vink, a pastor, but more so, a friend.  Shalom to you.- B.H.*

*To Myron, my best friend, and our sons Jacob and Myer, love you to the moon and back.-A.V.K.*

# Foreword

Christians of every nation and through all of time, bear an insatiable thirst for truth and grace, which tumble from the pages of Scripture. An encounter with the Holy Word of God is much like drinking seawater to quench one's thirst. For an instant the thirst is no more, then it comes raging back with a fury that is frightening. A taste of Truth, a swallow of Grace and one quickly learns that they must have more. An encounter with Jesus, the Word made Flesh, and they *need* more. Why else did Jesus' disciples walk away from everything in order to follow him?

The disciple John tells us why he wrote his portion of the Bible, *"These things are written that you may believe that Jesus is the Messiah, the Son of God, and that by believing you may have life in His name."*

In fact, the entire Bible is the story of Jesus:

> *There are lots of stories in the Bible, but all the stories are telling one Big Story. The Story of how God loves his children and comes to rescue them. It takes the whole Bible to tell this Story. And at the center of the Story, there is a baby. Every story in the Bible whispers his name. He is like the missing piece of a puzzle – the piece that makes all the other pieces fit together, and suddenly you see a beautiful picture.*

Last Advent season at the church I pastor in Visalia, California, we wanted to acknowledge that all of Scripture prepares us for the coming Messiah. We asked Blake Hiemstra to use the complete scope of Scripture to help us prepare for Christmas. His collection of twenty-five devotionals for Advent beautifully weave the story of Jesus into the New and Old Testaments. His writing, somehow witty yet solemn, is an example of how the Bible is intended to be read and thought about. Blake's devotions are an exercise in listening to how every story of Scripture whispers Jesus' name. Andrea Kamper, our congregation's Children's Ministry Director, and a gifted artist in her own right, painted a symbolic image to accompany and enhance each of the 25 devotionals. The resulting teamwork of pen and brush interlace story and image into a mosaic of a larger picture, the Big Picture story of Christmas.

Rev. Joel Renkema

# Introduction

As anyone who's walked this twirling planet for any length of time can attest, during the Christmas season the globe seems to make like a swiveling figure skater, spinning faster and faster, almost dizzyingly out of control. Cookies to bake. Presents to shake. Decorations to take. All, of course, before Christmas break. And those are just the things we plan for, besides the last-minute dinner invite or the visit from the long-lost, out-of-town relatives whose ten-minute drop-in turns into a three-hour exercise in patience.

In this general hubbub of the Christmas season, it often becomes more difficult to focus clearly. All of life's obligations, whether welcome or uninvited, sometimes work together to suffocate one's spirit, stifling the contemplation of the true Christ who is at the heart of Christmas.

As a Christian the only way to truly celebrate Christmas is to see this Christ. This book is a chance to encounter Christ and see how He's woven in and through every part of the greatest story ever told. It follows the tradition of the Jesse Tree, the idea of which comes from a verse in Isaiah. *"A shoot will come up from the stump of Jesse; from his roots a Branch will bear fruit."* In this passage God promises Israel that a Savior is coming from the line of Jesse, the father of David, who will sit on the throne forever. The Jesse Tree then is the symbol for how God worked through Jesse's line and through the whole scope of the Bible to prepare for the coming of the Messiah. This book allows you to think through God's wondrous ways in a fresh perspective, hopefully refreshing you once again for the Advent of the Christ-child.

It is our hope and dream that reading through these devotionals and contemplating the artwork, whether by yourself or with others, allow you to see the beauty, majesty and supremacy of Christ. We hope that you might grasp the holy beauty of the story of redemption, how every single page of the Word points to the Living Word who *"became flesh and made his dwelling among us."* And maybe, in some small way as you engage with heart and mind, your spirit might have the radiance of Moses when he came down from Mount Sinai because he'd had the authentic experience of *Glimpsing the Divine*.

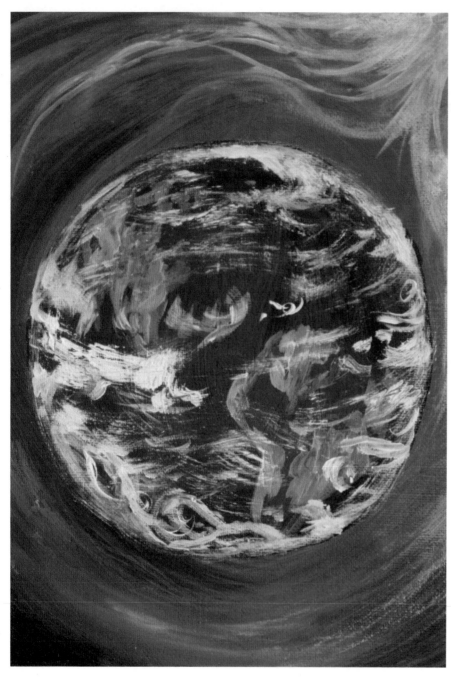

Imagine the scene played out in any living room in any house of any member of your church. Christmas Eve comes and gathered around a rapidly decaying pine sits an entire family, listening to the mellow voice of Bing Crosby, gazing in wonder at the twinkling lights and taking in the shiny rainbow of colors amassed in clumps of presents under the tree. In the center of it all sits a box slightly smaller than some European autos with a great, big bow.

Mom and Dad sit, side by side on the couch, knowing grins on their faces, delighting in the joy of showering their children with good gifts. They see their kids' eyes ablaze with wonder and mystery, wanting to know the contents of The Gift.

Essentially Genesis 1 paints the same scene. There's a flood of sparkling lights and a vast array of colors and sounds and wonders. And then there's the Father, taking in the scene and pronouncing it good. *"God saw all that he had made, and it was very good."* You might imagine God the Father taking it all in, seeing the delight and wonder and fruitfulness of creation, and smiling.

To put it simply, creation is a great, grand, glorious glad gift. Make no mistake. God didn't have to speak the beauty into place. He was neither bored nor lonely. He simply loved and wanted to create, to shower his creatures with the blessing of a great big Gift.

And just as this gift reverberated with the glory of God, so it gave a preview of the ultimate gift that is to come, one not wrapped in shiny cellophane, but swaddling cloths. One not nestled beneath a pine tree, but rather cradled in a wooden manger. It's the gift of a Father giving up that which is most precious to him, his only son.

As we look at the beautiful sights and sounds of creation this Christmas, may we remember the gift given at the dawn of time and the ultimate gift that Christmas celebrates.

---

## Let's Talk About It:

-What does today's painting show us about the Scripture passage?

-What's the best gift you've ever received? Given?

-How is creation a gift? How is Jesus a gift? What's the best way to celebrate and express gratitude this Christmas?

---

## Prayer:

*Father, thank you for creating us in your image and for loving us so much that you want to shower us with good gifts. Amen.*

One need not travel as far as a tropical rainforest or a tranquil, isolated beach to recapture the original Paradise. He or she only needs to journey as far as a local mall to enter the modern day essence of Eden known as Pottery Barn. The aroma of the divine wafts through the place; everything's perfectly arranged from the candles to the colors to the whole feng-shui phenomenon. One might half expect a Tree of Life replica to be for sale, though it'd probably be plastered with a price tag of $3499.00 in such a place. Apparently perfection's not cheap.

Now imagine Pottery Barn getting tagged by vandals followed by a category 5 hurricane, and you might be nearing a proper metaphor for the destruction and damage caused by the buying of a single lie in Genesis 3.

One lie and the delicious, dreamy, great, grand, glorious, glad gift of creation is tarnished and dirtied. One lie and relationships strain. One lie and there's no more teaching the world to sing in perfect harmony. One lie and the world is characterized by brokenness and desperation.

Sure, the simple act of eating a piece of fruit seems benign compared to the force of a hurricane, but it was entirely as destructive. And in the aftermath of disaster, there's a need to pick up the pieces and heal the brokenness. While a flood of Salvation Army workers might be able, in time, to put back together the pieces of a hurricane-ravaged community, there's only one way to restore the core of our lives and make wholeness a reality.

The truth is, every time in our lives that we choose self over others, we resound with ominous echoes of Adam and Eve's prideful purchase of the Big Lie. But every time we make the difficult phone call or offer the oh-so-needed hug to the grieving widow or choose to forgive instead of nursing a grudge, we put a few pieces back together and give a foretaste of what's to come; when the Great Restorer- Jesus Christ- who makes all things new- brings wholeness to a broken world.

## Let's Talk About It:

-What does today's painting show us about the Scripture passage?
-What was the big deal about one little piece of fruit?
-What are things that we do that contribute to the brokenness of our world? What are some things we can do to put the pieces back together?

## Prayer:

*Jesus, thank you for coming into this world to heal our hurts and fix the brokenness of our lives. We love you. Amen.*

While Noah and Mrs. Noah and company receive most of the press in this story, surely they weren't the only actors in this drama. In fact the very reason for the drama itself is because of the other players. *"God saw how corrupt the earth had become, for all the people on earth had corrupted their ways."* There's a whole population of renegades and hooligans for whom the cozy tale of bobbing up and down in the floating cypress-wood cocoon isn't reality. For them sheer terror characterizes this incident in human history.

We might imagine what happened as the *"floodgates of the heavens were opened."* The corrupt men and women of the earth, soaked and sodden, began to climb to higher ground. As water rose, men scaled mountains and scampered up trees. Desperately struggling to keep their heads above the waters closing in around them, perhaps the men got religious. Foxholes and dire straits tend to motivate in that regard. Before the waters completely swelled, a chorus of hysteric cries gets thrown to the heavens: "God, why have you forsaken us?"

While it would be wrong to draw a comparison between these wicked men and women and the Righteous One who actually uttered these words, the fact is that this is how God works. Through despair, destruction and death, He brings new life. In the midst of tragedy, God works. When it seems like hope abandons the world, God gives new hope.

The story of the great flood is one of God using destruction and terror to cleanse the earth and start anew. Picture the contrast between the pandemonium and terror of the flood with the new chapter that began as the door to the ark opened. Noah and the animals are met with enough verdant green to make Ireland jealous. Freshness, vibrancy, beauty- all of these greet Noah's eyes, perhaps reminiscent of the lushness of the now-forbidden garden of Eden.

And written in the sky in the first-ever recorded experience of high definition is a glowing rainbow, stretched across the heavens declaring the promise that not only will God never destroy the world in that way again, but also that the next time a cleansing happens, it won't be destructive. It will be redemptive. For Jesus Christ, the one for whom we wait and the one who we celebrate during Advent, will surely usher us into another new beginning at the end of time, a new beginning so glorious that the most brilliant rainbow is only the palest of foreshadowing of the beauty to come.

## Let's Talk About It:

-What does today's painting show us about the Scripture passage?
-Tell about a time in your life in which God made beauty out of ashes.
-What does the story of the flood foreshadow?

## Prayer:

*Father, thank you for your faithfulness, for your plan and for turning all of our mourning into dancing. Amen.*

We might dismiss the "babblers" in Genesis 11 as foolishly seeking that which cannot be sought. Obviously we can't get to heaven. We know that. We've learned the black page of the VBS tract by heart. *"For all have sinned and fall short of the glory of God."* Original sin. Total depravity. Yep. We've got it. We'd never arrange a church work day with enough pallets of bricks and enough wheelbarrows full of mortar to skyscrape our way to the pearly gates. That'd be asinine. We might bemoan the babblers as foolish, but the truth is we're pretty similar. Towers are passé, so ancient-world; the new edifice is the pedestal.

We tend to rank and put the saints among us on a pedestal, a little higher up than the rest. Let's play a little parlor game. Go around the table and name some folks who might be considered great. You know, the men and women who've done the extraordinary in the service of humanity, the ones who've loved their fellow man and lived lives that make the rest of the planet sit up and take notice. Yeah, do it right now. Go ahead. This book's not going anywhere . . .

Chances are good that names like Mother Teresa or the Reverend Billy Graham got bantered about. And there's no denying that they've lived extraordinary lives, using the gifts God gave them to do extraordinary acts of service in the world. Even in our own communities we do this. Mention the name of a local legend and just watch the awe and reverence flow into people's eyes. Start talking about a saintly woman and be prepared for tears. It's as if we see a giant ladder stretching from the bottom of the earth to the highest of heaven, and we plot each person we meet somewhere along the hierarchy of moral goodness. The greats we venerate, slotting them a dozen rungs up; the reprobates we denigrate, hanging them near the bottom.

The problem though isn't that we categorize; it's human nature to either chide or champion others. The error we make is in underestimating the size of the ladder that stretches heavenward. We plot greatness on a 40-foot extension ladder, which really would prove useless trying to stretch from rim to rim of the Grand Canyon, the size of the chasm between us and God, a chasm that we can't possibly traverse by ourselves. The truth is that when the original Christmas Day dawned, Jesus wasn't just born in a manger; he climbed down from heaven on a ladder, all the way to the very bottom, where we live. And while we might like to picture him picking us up and carrying us up the ladder to glory, the truth is that when he reached out his arms on the cross, his stretched, tattered body became the ladder, allowing us to do what the babblers couldn't do on their own: enter the glorious presence of the living God.

Kind of makes you want to sing *"Gloria in excelsis Deo"* with a little more gusto, doesn't it?

## Let's Talk About It:

-What does today's painting show us about the Scripture passage?

-What's the tallest building you've ever seen?

-Why did God confuse the language of the babblers and thwart their plans?

## Prayer:

*Jesus, thank you for loving us enough to offer your body to open the way for us to be with you forever. We love you. Amen.*

Carol craned her head sideways, trying to get a little bit better look at the ultrasound monitor. She couldn't believe it. She and Steve. Here again. Already blessed with six beautiful children, the possibility of being pregnant once again wasn't welcomed with open arms. They both, literally and especially mentally, were done. At 35 years old and with the youngest already out of diapers, they were ready for the next stage of life that didn't involve a high chair or a pack 'n' play.

Steve stood next to the examining room table, gently caressing Carol's hand, watching the scene unfold before them.

"Well," said Dr. Meyers, "It looks like you're pregnant . . ."

"That's what we kind of thought was hap-," Carol

tried to say but she cut off Dr. Meyers, who wasn't finished.

". . . with quadruplets."

Tears welled up in Carol's eyes as she brought one hand to cover her mouth. With the other she reached to squeeze Steve's. She couldn't reach Steve's hand though as she looked and saw it on top of Steve's passed-out body on the floor.

Sometimes the news, even though it's good, is almost too much to handle. It's like trying to stuff 4 gigs of joy into our feeble 256 megabyte brains. We just can't fathom it. Sometimes blessings overwhelm our ability to comprehend the magnitude of our God.

Consider Abram and Sarai. The Lord comes to their tent and offers the news that the whole world will be blessed through them. "Sounds great, God, but by the way, you do realize that I'm as old as these hills here, right?" He must have thought, "How could God make this happen?"

The good news is that the message the Lord shared with Abram and Sarai is the same one that Jesus gives to us. He's the one who *"is able to do immeasurably more than all we ask or imagine. . ."* He came into this world so that the blessing given to Abram might be fulfilled through him. That all who call on his name might be saved. And this blessing and his plan to redeem his people are way bigger than what we can truly understand. The question is whether or not we realize it.

When a neighboring church reports record attendance and the lost being saved in droves, what's our response? Do we drop to our knees in praise and gratitude, or do we think that if we had a little more contemporary worship style or a different youth guy, we'd have the same thing happen.

Abram's response to the Blessing? *"So Abram went."* Okay, God. You want to bless the world through me? Okay. The Christ that came into this world, the one through whom all men on earth can be saved, wants the same obedience from us.

| Let's Talk About It: |
|---|

-What does today's painting show us about the Scripture passage?

-In your own life how have you seen God's plan being so much more than you could even imagine?

-What practical implications do these words have? *"And all peoples on earth will be blessed through you."*

| Prayer: |
|---|

*Jesus, it is only through you and through your name that all peoples on earth can be blessed. Thank you for being the Way, the Truth and the Life. Amen.*

Certain hymns have a rather Pavlovian power. Play a few bars of "He Leadeth Me" and watch the eyes moisten up and down the pews. Tickle the ivory to the tune of "Amazing Grace" and get out the Kleenex.

Some songs though go the distance, having the ability to pluck the heart strings like a master harpist. When the third verse of "How Great Thou Art" crescendos, our emotions carry a weight born of love. *"And when I think, that God his son not sparing, sent Him to die, I scarce can take it in. That on a cross, my burden gladly bearing, He bled and died, to take away my sin."* Anyone who's ever held his own newborn can't quite fathom that type of love. It evokes trembling.

Similarly we read the story of Abraham and Isaac climbing the mountain and struggle to grasp it. It's like hearing that the couple who've been wanting a child for years and years finally got pregnant . . . and then miscarried again. *Are you sure, God?*

*Really?* Like learning that the cancer returned. Again. *What, God? How come . . .*

After waiting for a son for the entire duration of the 100 Years War, Abraham finally cradles flesh of his flesh in his hands. Tears surely overwhelm his eyes. Gratitude floods his soul. All his blessings, all his wealth are nothing compared to the joy of holding life in his arms.

Surely Abraham and Isaac shared a bond as the boy grew. Hunting together. Wrestling. Roaming the estate side by side. True father-son camaraderie. It makes sense that Isaac lived up to his name and produced belly-shaking laughter.

Then the bottom falls out. God directs Abraham to sacrifice this blessing on an altar. As they climb the mountain, Abraham's heart turns leaden. The gravitas of such an act weighs on his shoulders. With tears cascading down his cheeks, he ties Isaac up and closes his eyes one final time in a desperate plea to the God who bade him to do this unthinkable deed. As he opens his eyes to the deafening silence, he raises the knife slowly, gingerly, and readies himself to plunge it into his beloved son. With trembling frame and tears dripping onto Isaac, he hears the booming, melodious voice of God, "Don't do it, Abraham." We might imagine the convulsions that seize Abraham as he embraces Isaac on the altar, realizing that his son will live.

God doesn't say it verbatim, but the story shouts it: It's not now, but the time will come when an only, beloved son will climb on the altar and be the sacrificial lamb. And while we struggle to fathom the depths of obedience that propel a father to raise the knife against his own son, we marvel and quiver at the even greater love- the love that drives a Father not to raise the knife, but rather to turn his back in silence as his only beloved Son gives his life for the entire world.

That's a silence that only the deepest love can produce. That's the love that the Father has for you.

---

## Let's Talk About It:

-What does today's painting show us about the Scripture passage?
-What's the greatest sacrifice you've made for others?
-How does the story of Abraham and Isaac point to Jesus?

---

## Prayer:

*Father, we marvel at the love you have for us, that you would give up your only Son that we may have life. Thank you. Amen.*

The forces of evil enjoyed quite the renaissance in the story of Joseph that unfolds in the latter chapters of Genesis. Hatred, Betrayal, Greed, Abuse, Slavery, Unjust Imprisonment, Sexual Immorality- all of these despicable characters play a role in this drama. Surely the wicked powers that be must have anticipated a complete victory for the dark side. The plot's corkscrews and double flips led to the poignant moment when Joseph-the protagonist-stands before the eleven brothers who contemplated murder before selling their little bro to a pack of hairy nomads in the middle of the desert. Surely, thought the forces of evil, this would be the grand finale. After all that he'd been through, he'll reach for the biggest club in the arsenal of evil: Revenge.

It's a similar situation to the predicament faced by Edmond Dantes in Alexander Dumas' *The Count of Monte Cristo*. Betrayed by Fernand, his best friend and by others closest to him and thrown in a cistern of a prison where he's beaten and basically left for dead, Edmond faces a future bleaker than a snowball in summer. Only through ingenuity and divine intervention does he escape and manage to rise to a position of fabulous wealth and power. Entrenched in his new position of regal authority, with his discarded life miraculously returned to him, he faces a similar choice: gratefully live out his new life as a servant or choose to pursue those who betrayed him and make them pay. He takes door number two, and the fervor for revenge seizes him, driving him onward until all his enemies' lives crumble or end. (And the villagers of the hamlet of Evil rejoice.)

For Joseph, with the treasury of Egypt at his disposal and Pharaoh's backing, revenge was easily attainable and perhaps tempting. And to those of us watching the plot-line unfurl, revenge might seem justifiable. His own flesh and blood sold him into slavery. It's a bit more heinous crime than giving the silent treatment or locking the little bro in a closest for a while, as we might do to a pesky younger sibling.

Instead of reaching for revenge, Joseph picks up the olive branch. He plays the card for which there is no possible answer from the forces of evil. Where they erred, he does the divine: he forgives. And it's a forgiveness born out of the realization that our God takes all the evil thrown our way and uses it for good. *"You intended to harm me, but God intended it for good to accomplish what is now being done, the saving of many lives."* Nothing thwarts the powers of evil quite like forgiveness and an eternal perspective.

The story of Joseph is a simple foreshadowing of yet another Prince, one who unjustly faces death at the hands of evil men yet divinely chooses to forgive. *"Father, forgive them, for they do not know what they are doing".* And this Prince, the Prince of all Peace, takes that which is intended for evil- the cross, the instrument of torture that might seem as out of place in a sanctuary as a swastika in a synagogue- and uses it for ultimate good, the saving of the human race.

## Let's Talk About It:

-What does today's painting show us about the Scripture passage?

-When have you been persecuted and reached for revenge? When have you been persecuted but chose to forgive?

-Which one taught you more?

## Prayer:

*Jesus, as we look to the cross, help us to see the choice you made to forgive, that we might have life. Thank you for showing us the power of forgiveness. In your Name, Amen.*

Yesteryear seems like forever ago. Prosperity retreats farther and farther into the rearview mirror. For these Israelites the memory of Joseph on the throne as Pharaoh's #2 fades with each succeeding generation. Of course, it's not like they have the leisure to reminisce. Feverishly stirring the mortar in the shadow of a mountainous Egyptian slave-driver tends to prohibit the nostalgic reveries. Reality for the nation of Israel is the cold, hard world of slavery, life inside the blackness of a tunnel with nary a speck of light in eyesight. Of course, our God does his best work in the dark.

Fortunately for the Israelites and for us, our God is a God of predictable creativity. The word "predictable" might seem to be a stumbling block to some. How can you say that God- the King eternal, immortal, invisible, the only

God- can be "predictable"? Ultimately the story of the Bible is that of a loving Father redeeming his children, of him bringing them back to himself. Throughout the narratives in the pages of the Bible, this much is constant, even predictable: God is going to save his children. He's God. He can't not save his children any more than we could keep ourselves from throwing our bodies in front of a car to save our own children.

That end though might get accomplished through means as creative as, well, defeating an army with a threadbare force and some jars and trumpets or encircling a city until its walls crumble or, well, painting a doorframe with the blood of a lamb. He is the *Creator*, after all.

Thus, when his people cry out for deliverance in the midst of their enslavement, he's going to save them. He might use the means of a burning bush and ten apocalyptic plagues to bring the Egyptians to the point where they beg the Israelites to leave, but there's no doubt that he will save his people. He can't help but redeem them.

Another word for "predictable" might be immutable or unchangeable. He's God today as he was God yesterday. When the last and deadliest of the plagues descends on the land, God saves the firstborns among the Israelites by the sacrifice of a lamb's blood on the doorframes of their homes. When His creation groans under the weight of sin, God again saves his people by the blood of a lamb, the spotless Lamb of God, shed on the cross.

As we anticipate the coming of the Christ this season, maybe we'd do well to realize that at Christmas, God did simply the same thing he did for the Israelites, the same thing he's always done: predictably carrying out his plan of redemption for his beloved children in the most creative of ways. Even through a baby who's *"Born a child and yet a King."*

---

## Let's Talk About It:

-What does today's painting show us about the Scripture passage?

-How in your life has God saved you in remarkably wonderful, unique ways?

-In what ways are we enslaved just like the Israelites were?

-Why was Jesus' sacrifice on the cross necessary? Couldn't we just each kill another lamb as a sacrifice?

---

## Prayer:

*Father, your love is amazing. Thank you that you love us and have authored the greatest rescue story that we could ever imagine. Amen.*

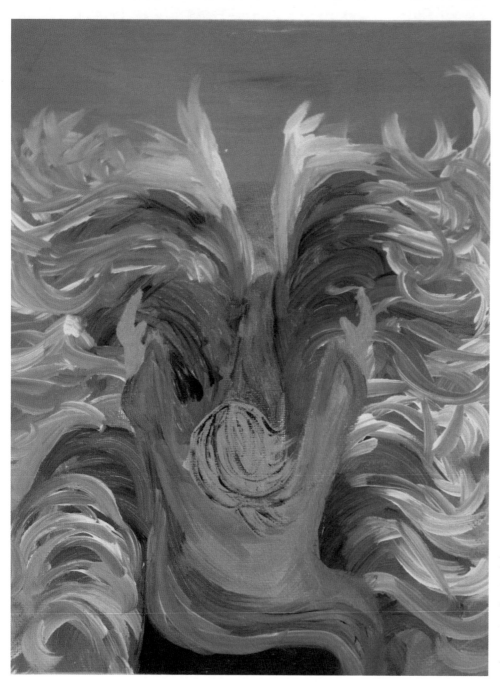

We know this scene well. It's Friday night, the work week is done and it's time for some entertainment. All eyes soak in the drama that comes to life on the plasma. In the story that unfolds, a vibrant young lady on the medical field catches the eye of the crusty, cantankerous fighter pilot with an attitude. Her love melts the curmudgeon's heart and thus begins a romance so passionate it makes Romeo and Juliet's seem platonic by comparison. On the eve of their wedding he takes her soaring through the heavens in his twin engine fighter plane, but crisis looms. Both engines fail. Tension mounts as the plane descends, spiraling towards certain death. They scramble about the plane, looking, pleading, hoping . . . even in the midst of no hope. They look into each other's eyes, panicked and scared. No words are spoken; instead, they continue their desperate plight. As the freefall continues they pry off an electrical panel to discover a single parachute. Arguing ensues until finally in one last, sweeping move, he straps on the parachute, opens the door, grabs her around the waist and jumps. Clutching each other like human life preservers, they magically float to safety on the ground. (Then the credits roll, the women gush with tears . . . and the pastor has next week's sermon illustration.)

It's basically the same dire scenario that the Israelites found themselves trapped in towards the middle of Exodus. On the run they face a seemingly impenetrable, flowing wall. They look back and see their enemies gaining. Terrified, they panic. Desperation seizes them. They wish for the unthinkable. *"It would have been better for us to serve the Egyptians."* Hopeless times wreak havoc on sound minds. Fortunately for them, when God's people get backed into a corner, God simply splits the corner in two and directs a divine escape route.

We see the same thing in our lives. Salvation springs out of hopeless causes. We hear the word "terminal" and then doctors can find no trace of the cancer. The word "divorce" gets uttered and then a renewed commitment to making it work follows. Foreclosure looms until an unexpected check comes in the mail.

God saves his people. God works in miraculous ways to deliver his chosen. Maybe through the faithfulness of a prostitute, maybe through the final obedience of an eyeless Atlas- however it happens, the fact is that God saves his people. His glory demands it. *"But I will gain glory for myself through Pharaoh and all his army, and the Egyptians will know that I am the Lord."*

Yes, God provides the way for salvation for his people. Except, of course, when the way can't be found. When our hands rise and the waters don't move. When the shackles of sin enslave us and extinguish all hope.

In those, the most dire of circumstances, God doesn't just make a way, he himself becomes the way. *"I am the Way and the Truth and the Life."* When faith dies, hope incarnates. Living hope takes on flesh and lives and dies, and it's not the waters of the Red Sea that get split in two; it's the temple veil that gets divinely ripped, allowing us, in Jesus' death, to pass through death to the glory and freedom of eternal life on the other side. And that rescue is more beautiful than any parachute can ever deliver.

## Let's Talk About It:

-What does today's painting show us about the Scripture passage?

-What's one time in your life in which hope seemed elusive and yet God saved you?

-Why does Jesus say, "I am the Way and the Truth and the Life"? (Hint- what comes after that line?)

## Prayer:

*Father, no matter the troubles we face or the trials of this place, you always make a way, each and every day. We love you. Amen.*

*M*y Dearest Children,

My love for you is endless. You are my beloved. There's no limit to the lengths I'll go to show the depths of my love. I love you more than you'll ever understand. When you cradle a newborn in your arms or embrace a child, you get the faintest wisp of the deep love I have for you. Although the whole world is mine, you are my special people, the holy nation that I love.

I want so much to live in harmony with you. I want our love to be so great that the rest of the world takes notice, that they see the deep love that we share and know that you are special.

I want the best for you. I want your lives to be special and unique and distinct. As the crown of my creation, you are blessed. As my holy people, a kingdom of priests, I'm giving you a special plan for how to live so that you can live the most peaceful, joyful lives possible. Because you're mine, because you belong to me, I want your lives to be worthy of the special relationship that we have.

*You are the most special people on earth, and I'm your Father. Relish me and no other as God, and I'll treasure you and spill my glory on you. Look to nothing else but me as your great provider.*

*I know each and every one of you by name, and I love it when you call me by my name. Talk to me all the time. I love it. Use my name. I love hearing it. Speak it gently, boldly, peacefully, quietly, in times of joy, in times of desperation. I love it when you call me.*

*Know that I created you to be just like me, to love to create and then to enjoy the blessing of rest. Luxuriate in that rest. Spend time with me and just be quiet every week. It'll be so nice to relax together.*

*Just as you and I have a special relationship as a daddy and his children, I want you to enjoy that special bond with each other. I've given you some pretty awesome people to act like me in your lives. Love 'em as much as you can. Lavish them with kisses and hugs. Love your moms and dads the same way you love me.*

*There's so much more I could say. There's nothing I love more than seeing my children living life fully together. I love seeing you living together. Love life together. Play, work, dance, sing, enjoy it all. Love each other. Speak gently and truly to each other. Share everything. Be happy just being together. Value each other and live in peace together.*

*Now I know that everything's not perfect. As much as I love you completely, I know that there will be times when you can't or don't love me back. And it will break my heart. Truly it will. But you know how much I love you? In order to keep on living in our special relationship, one day I'm going to give my very own son whom I love more than life itself for your lives. I can't stand the thought of living apart from you. And as much as it will pain me to see my own son suffer, I'll do it because I love you. And you know what? He does too. And you know what else? Because he loves you, we all get to live together forever and ever and ever as one big, huge happy family, singing and dancing and laughing and loving life. I sure love you.*

*Love, Father*

## Let's Talk About It:

-What does today's painting show us about the Scripture passage?

-What's the most touching letter you've ever received?

-How much does the Father love you?

## Prayer:

*Father, there's nothing that compares with your love. Thank you for lavishing it on us and loving us so much that you'd give your own Son so that we can be with you forever. In His Name, Amen.*

Looking back on the whole of David's life, it's easy to see how he hoisted the scepter. If ancient Israel had a *Renaissance Man Today* publication, he'd surely be the poster boy. First, he's a warrior. A sword in his hand fit like it was meant to be there. Second, he's a leader. Anyone who's got a few inches of press in II Samuel describing his own "Mighty Men" surely knew a thing about leadership. Third, he's fearless. He tangos with a nine-foot leviathan in human form when no one else goes near the ring. More than that, he's cultivated the noble art of writing, penning the most beautiful worship poems in the history of the world. Plus, he's the total package, combining physical prowess and creative passion with mad, wicked skills on the harp. He undoubtedly could do it all. It's easy to see why he won the general election in a landslide.

Well, it's easy to see, except that way back at the beginning when God sent Samuel on the mission to anoint King #2, he didn't care about David's reflection in the mirror or the number of friends he had in his Facebook account. In fact, when Samuel went searching, he came up empty because he thought that pedigree mattered to God. When Jesse parades his sons before Samuel, he thought surely that it'd be one of David's older brothers who would get the nod. God swiftly answers Samuel. *"Do not consider his appearance or his height, for I have rejected him. The LORD does not look at the things people look at. People look at the outward appearance, but the LORD looks at the heart."*
For God, it's always, completely, only . . . about the heart.

There's no coincidence that God's chosen instrument to lead his people is the only man in Scripture described by God as *"a man after my own heart."* For God, it's always about the heart.

The same is true with us. Actions may charm the public, but the motivation behind them is what stirs the heart of God. A chic wardrobe may turn the heads of the masses, but the heart's beauty is what turns the head of the Father. He keeps not a ledger of our assets nor a photo album of our vacations. As David's wise son explains, *"A person may think their own ways are right, but the Lord weighs the heart."*

David wasn't the typical choice for royalty. He was the smallest of the bunch, the one no one expected. Likewise, when God sent the promised one to take the throne that David once occupied, he sent one that people may not have expected. As Isaiah explains, *"He had no beauty or majesty to attract us to him, nothing in his appearance that we should desire him."* But just as David was a man after God's own heart, the promised Messiah was a man *with* God's own heart.

And it's that King with God's own heart who still reigns on the throne today, and he shall reign forever and ever, alleluia, alleluia. Amen.

## Let's Talk About It:

-What does today's painting show us about the Scripture passage?
-What was it about David that made God pick him as the next king?
-What makes your heart look a little bit more like God's?

## Prayer:

*Father, we pray that our hearts might beat in time with yours. Give us a heart for the things of this world that will never pass away. Amen.*

Though they dwell in vastly different realms, essentially antique dealers and insurance agents spend their time doing the same thing: trying to plaster a price tag on the priceless. For the antique dealer it might be endeavoring to figure out a suitable price for a circa 1890's vintage dresser that's unblemished in form or appearance. For the insurance agent it might be seeking to estimate the value of a possible severed index finger to a concert pianist. For either the task of calculating the incalculable seems nearly impossible.

Essentially it's the same thing that Naaman tried to do in II Kings 5, with no success. A valiant soldier and commander of the king's army, Naaman seemingly had it all, except, of course, for what he had all over: leprosy. He's plagued with the dreaded disease of antiquity for which no human remedy can alleviate the pain nor cheer up the bleak future. Given his position of power, he's not accustomed to listening to the advice of the hired help, but desperation often changes one's M.O.  He hears the counsel of his wife's servant girl and goes in search of this prophet, clutching something that leprosy victims don't normally carry: hope.

Eventually Naaman finds Elisha and is so enamored with the possibility of healing . . . that he decides to forsake Elisha's prescription and stomp away angry.  Again, a servant intervenes and steers Naaman towards the Jordan. (It makes one wonder if there's not a deeper theme in this passage about the role of the servant in the playing out of salvation.)  Naaman takes seven dips in the Jordan and rises out of the water clean and new.  The leprosy has disappeared.  Salvation, granted.

His skin smooth once again, Naaman does what we'd do.  He pulls out his checkbook.  He prepares to write a big one with enough zeroes to right a recession.  Elisha will have none of this.  *As surely as the Lord lives, whom I serve, I will not accept a thing.*  Elisha instructs Naaman, as well as those reading along at home, that while salvation might be precious and priceless, it's still a free gift of a good God.

The gift of new life, of salvation, is free to all who seek it.  It matters not the status nor the assets of the seekers.  As the prophet Isaiah says, *"Come, all you who are thirsty, come to the waters; and you who have no money, come, buy and eat!  Come, buy wine and milk without money and without cost."*  Surely at Christmas it's easy to understand the nature of the most blessed gift ever given, the gift of God's own Son.

The question is whether or not we'll freely receive it.  Of course, you might scream.  To not do so would be preposterous.  Notice the question though is whether we'll "freely" receive it.  Like Naaman, do we want to accept the gift, but still slide the check across the counter?  Do we think that if we're really, really good, maybe God will love us more?  Maybe our exemplary lives will make the transaction a little less one-sided?

To celebrate the ultimate gift is to realize the zeroes stacked up in our moral assets column and to realize our complete dependence on the Son who freely gives us life.  To realize that we're lost until we're found and forgiven by the Father.  No insurance agent alive could put a price tag on that kind of priceless grace.

## Let's Talk About It:

-What does today's painting show us about the Scripture passage?

-If God doesn't want us to earn or pay for salvation, why does he want us to tithe?

-How is Jesus the ultimate gift?

## Prayer:

*Dear Jesus, it is only through the giving of your life for us that we might be saved.  Thank you for the free gift of salvation that's priceless. In your Name, Amen.*

# Day 13 - *Cleaning the Closets of Our Hearts* (read II Kings 22 & 23:21-23)

It's a process that every single one of us goes through at some point during the fall. Somewhere between the uttering of "Trick or treat" and the singing of *"Yea, Lord, we greet thee, born this happy morning,"* we reach into the closets and attics of our lives and pull out all the accoutrements of Christmas. Lights, tinsel, Nativity scenes. Candy canes, ornaments, and everything in between. The go-getters get it going early, playing nonstop Christmas tunes weeks before the Thanksgiving turkey gets carved. Others try to delay the inevitable, failing to embrace the yuletide until the last possible minute. No matter when, it's clear that the season of Advent is one of preparation, of getting ready for the celebration that is to come.

However, as the young king Josiah discovered, having the Word of God cause a holy ruckus on the inside is a far more important cataclysm than anything that happens on the surface area of our lives.

Even though he took the throne at the ripe old age of eight, Josiah still *did what was right in the eyes of the Lord.*" Merely a decade into his reign, he orders the temple to be restored and cleaned out. In the process the Book of the Law is discovered. When Josiah hears the Word and realizes the sin of omission that he's committed by not obeying the "words of this book," he tears his robes. He's distraught over his sin and the sins of his people. The Word of God dissects his heart. Such is the case when we have a divine encounter with the living and holy Word of Truth. It rightly causes us to evaluate our motivations and our actions. In short, to check our hearts. Undoubtedly the temple repairs were put on hold by Josiah until the heart restoration came to completion.

We all have times in our lives when we lose sight of what's important. When we forget the heart of the matter. When we obsess over the external instead of the internal. When we care more about the light on the top of the Christmas tree than the light shining in our hearts. In this case Josiah's lesson is pretty powerful: to abandon the Word of God and to forsake the condition of our hearts is worthy of tearing one's robes and falling on our knees in repentance before the Lord.

Christmas is a time of expectation and anticipation. We passionately sing, *"Come thou long expected Jesus."* We do much to prepare the adornments of our lives for the coming of the Messiah. Maybe as we unpack the embellishments of Christmas, we need to recklessly unpack the Word of God and clean out the closets of our hearts. Maybe we're not fully ready for the coming of the Savior unless the Word of God has intersected our hearts and dropped us to our knees before the throne.

Maybe when that happens, we're ready, even if the egg nog's not yet poured.

## Let's Talk About It:

-What does today's painting show us about the Scripture passage?
-What do you need to do in order to get ready for Christmas?
-When's the last time you've *"torn your robe"* after having an encounter with the Word of Truth?

## Prayer

*Father, thanks for the joy of Christmas and the spirit of expectation. Prepare our hearts for the coming of the Messiah. In your Name, Amen.*

Psalm 23 is the ultimate in comfort food for the soul. Mental pictures of lush green and placid waters float through our heads. Cozy scenes of sheep and shepherd ambling side by side over the hills and valleys of life kindle feelings of contentment and fulfillment. Even the powers of darkness can't sully this picturesque contemplation because the shepherd is present through the deepest of valleys. At the end of the Psalm blessed eternity awaits, along with goodness and love and all the other blessings of life with the shepherd.

Yes, it's the ultimate comfort and feel-good Psalm . . . except, of course, when it's not. . .

*When the parched wasteland of our lives in this world makes us beg for any hint of green.*

*When the storms rage and the personal demons thunder, drowning out any wisp of stillness.*

*When the paths we tread teem with treachery and deceit, miles away from any paths of righteousness.*

*When the shadow of death looms a little too close for comfort and we're not sure if we'll have to traverse that ravine sooner than we'd like.*

*When the pangs of loneliness claw at our hearts, needling us, making us long for a phone call or a simple hello.*

*When the junk we ingest fails to quell the gnawing hunger we have for significance and recognition.*

*When despair swallows optimism and the trials of tomorrow morning engulf any possible longing for eternity.*

Some of us are there, in that place of hurt and loneliness. Not wanting to be there, but there nonetheless. Powerless. Forlorn. Frightened. And abandoned. Kind of like a dirty, aimless sheep . . . without a shepherd.

And it's in that place of misery and dejection that, more than anything else, we need Christmas. No, we don't need the endless list of social engagements or the stress of extra family gatherings. It's not even the hallowed radiance of a candlelight service that we need. It's what Christmas offers to one and all, at every point along the journey on this earth: The Promise. Christmas Day gave birth to the ultimate Promise, that the child squirming in the manger is not just a child. That this baby, slightly smaller than a newborn lamb, is not just any shepherd, but the Good Shepherd. He's the one who's able to not only walk with us through the droughts of life, but also the one who'll lovingly hoist us on his shoulders when the hurts of life make the walking impossible. He's the one who knows each one of us by name and won't slumber until we're safe by his side. And above all else he's the one who *"lays down his life for the sheep."*

It is this Promise that Christmas brings, and it makes us realize that no matter how distant we might feel from the Father, however unattainable the quiet waters might seem, the Good Shepherd will lead his flock back to where we belong, nestled next to God's heart.

---

## Let's Talk About It:

-What does today's painting show us about the Scripture passage?

-What do you know about sheep?

-Why is Jesus the great Promise at Christmas?

---

## Prayer:

*Father, as lonely, misguided sheep, there's nothing we need more than guidance and love. Thank you for giving us Jesus as the Good Shepherd, to protect us and to lead us. In His Name, Amen.*

In the sometimes miry world of national politics, there's one time in every four-year cycle that's relatively free of acrimony and disdain. At each party's general nominating convention, there's usually a spirit of optimism, free from the contempt and venom that often characterize party politics in this country. It's fun to imagine what might happen if Isaiah were to take the stage at a national political convention as the keynote speaker and give the message of chapter 9. His address might inspire the masses, at least until he comes to the end.

*Friends, Oklahomans, countrymen, lend me your ears. This long period of darkness is coming to an end. The light will shine once again. It's time for rejoicing and dancing. It's time for celebration. No more will the yoke of oppression burden your shoulders. Warfare shall cease. Peace shall reign.* (Thunderous applause surely would follow, but Isaiah isn't quite done.)

*For to us one is given who will be the most high, the one who we'll exult. The world has never seen a ruler with his equal. He'll be the ultimate king, the consummate leader. With justice and integrity he will rule. There will be no end to his governing nor to the peace that he will usher in.* (Again, thunderous applause and perhaps even a few "Here, heres.")

*But make no mistake. This time of peace and harmony and justice is not just for this country; it's for the world. This king will usher in a time of unity and harmony with all peoples on earth for this time and forevermore. No longer will we battle with others across the globe. No longer shall we think solely of what's good for America. We'll only think of the kingdom of the one to come, whose rule shall never end.* (A much quieter smattering of applause ensues.)

*And what shall make this new creation happen? What shall bring about this change? Is it the grassroots fervor of devoted volunteers? Is it the platform of a political party? Is it the passion of the liberal left? Is it your undying ardor for change? NO! It's none of those. This new kingdom will happen only, , because of the zeal of the Lord Almighty. It is only the jealous love that he has for his people that drives him to make this happen. Because of Him, for Him, through Him, a new kingdom shall reign.*

Isaiah's message, the one that we sing of and celebrate and put on the insides of Christmas cards, is the one that makes Christmas worthy of the celebration that we give it. For it gives us a glimpse into the heart of God, who loves not just one nation, but the entire world that he created. The Son that he gives is the hope for not just our community, nor our nation, but the hope of the entire world. To celebrate Christmas and to celebrate the Christ-child is to have a kingdom mindset, knowing that Christ's reign *"from that time on and forever"* is one that will move all peoples on earth to bend their knees and bow at his throne.

---

## Let's Talk About It:

-What does today's painting show us about the Scripture passage?

-What is the "zeal of the Lord Almighty" that Isaiah refers to and what does it have to do with us?

-How is Christmas a time for prophecy?

---

## Prayer:

*Father, all good that happens on this earth is through you and because of you. Thank you for your zeal that loves us and brought us your Son. Amen.*

Quite the strange phenomenon occurs every year around the first of December. People change. The convenience store clerk who's usually the reincarnation of Ebenezer Scrooge suddenly turns all Mary Poppins, cheerfully exhorting you to "Have a nice day." Merging onto the freeway, normally an exercise in white-knuckled survival of the fittest, becomes instead a mingling with merry motorists, as road rage gives way to an epidemic of common courtesy. It's what people call the expression of the Christmas spirit. It's as if the whole world joins hands together singing in perfect harmony, as if bipartisan politicians share a malt in a soda shop. It's beautiful. It's delightful. It's unnatural.

One of the drawbacks of living in a world marred with the stain of sin is that the longer we dwell in the darkness, the more normal shadow-living feels. We exist in the confines of a room lit by candlelight, accustomed to twilight, ignorant of the invention of fluorescent bulbs. We accept strained family relationships as the norm, moving neither to change them nor thinking that it's even possible. We turn a blind eye to underage drinking, rolling the eyes and saying, "Kids will be kids." We feel powerless to make any substantive changes in our lives. "Transformation" and "reformation" may be catchy buzzwords in our community, but "resignation" is often the de facto descriptor of our lives.

In this spirit of grave acceptance of the world, we desperately need the vision of Isaiah 11. We need the glimpse of the power of the Messianic age. Isaiah shows us that the coming of the Christ-child means no more business as usual. All that we know and accept of this world will be turned upside down. Christ will usher in a time of such peace and safety that the world we know will be but a faint reflection of the glorious new reality that we'll know then. Wolves will live with lambs. Leopards and goats will lie down together. Kids will play harmoniously with vipers. Children will honor parents. Relationships, restored. Even Democrats and Republicans will play nice with each other.

The Christmas spirit that's palpable in the checkout lines of our lives is simply a foretaste of a life to come that's so much greater than we realize. The shoot from Jesse that comes in triumph and power into this world will make all things new, taking away the tears, filling our lives with the richness of a new creation. Ponder that the next time you hear "Have a nice day" coming from the most unexpected source.

It's what the characters at the end of C.S. Lewis' *The Last Battle* experienced, the "more" that the next world has to offer. A unicorn utters the foretaste that Christmas gives: *"I have come home at last! This is my real country! I belong here. This is the land I have been looking for all my life, though I never knew it 'til now. The reason why we loved the old Narnia is that it sometimes looked a little like this. Bree-hee-hee! Come further up, come further in!"* Jesus came to bring us the life that we've been looking for all our lives but never could find.

## Let's Talk About It:

-What does today's painting show us about the Scripture passage?
- In what ways in your life have you simply settled for the darkened, shadowy version of what could be?
- What areas of your life need the transforming power of Christmas?

## Prayer:

*Father, thank you that sending your Son into this world changes everything and gives us hope. Lead us, Lord, in the way everlasting. Amen.*

If we wanted a little Christmas inspiration from the Bible, we'd know where to go. We'd thumb pages until we get to the second chapter of Luke and then uncork the nostalgia. Visions of Sunday school programs and Nativity scenes would flood our minds. Shepherds and swaddling cloths. Choruses of *"Gloria in excelsis Deo."* The picture of mother Mary serenely nestled with the baby Jesus as she ponders everything that's happened. Maybe even an idyllic image of lowing cattle, even if we're not sure what exactly cattle do when they "low," except that it causes the baby to wake but not cry.

Yes, these are the pictures of Christmas that touch our hearts, that make us feel cozy. But it's not a complete picture, which makes it not completely accurate. It's the same vision of Christmas that's shared by millions of non-Christians because it doesn't necessarily include the Father's perspective . . . found in Isaiah 53.

When God the Father contemplates Christmas, he doesn't just see the starry night flooded with the brilliance of the heavenly hosts. He can't see the rough wood of the manger without seeing the splintery timber of the cross. In His eyes there's no separation between Christmas and Easter. Yes, his only beloved son was born amid the fanfare of angels, but his heralded birth only began the countdown to his inevitable death and resurrection.

Though truly laudable and fervor-producing, Christmas exists as only a part of the process, a step in the salvation of His people. That plan gets detailed in Isaiah 53, and it's a plan that's beautiful, not for the warm fuzzies it produces, but for the deep love it evidences. Only a God like our God could hatch a plan for the salvation of his beloved creatures that involves his own son running the gauntlet in the cold, dark confines of earth. Only a God like ours could plan for his own son to be *"despised and rejected by mankind."* Only a God like ours could watch his own son be one *"from whom people hide their faces."* Only a God like ours could envision his own son being *"pierced for our transgressions . . . (and) crushed for our iniquities."* Only a God like ours could foresee the very people he's trying to save turning their backs on his son and then still laying *"on him the iniquity of us all."*

Maybe the angels in the heavens celebrating the birth of Jesus were not just lauding the arrival of the Savior of the world. Maybe they also were trumpeting the love of a Father who loves all his creatures so much that he's willing to initiate the unleashing of a rescue plan so wonderfully sacrificial, that it's the most beautiful story ever told.

## Let's Talk About It:

-What does today's painting show us about the Scripture passage?
-There's already a song with this title, but try putting it in your own words: How deep is the Father's love for us?
-Why must a celebration of Christmas include Isaiah 53?

## Prayer:

*Father, again and again, we're reminded of the depths of your love. Thank you for loving us so much that you endured the sacrifice of your own Son so that we could be saved. In your grace, Amen.*

When Jean Valjean finally tastes freedom after nineteen years behind bars for the simple act of stealing a loaf of bread and repeated attempts at escape, his heart has hardened so completely that he can't freely breathe the air of liberation. The title character in Victor Hugo's *Les Miserables*, Valjean's heart continues to harden as he encounters no small lack of hospitality. Being an ex-con in a weary world offers few opportunities to experience the kindness of strangers. He finally feels the compassion of a man of the cloth as the Bishop of Digne takes him in and gives him shelter. Valjean responds to this kindness . . . by stealing the Bishop's silver and taking off. His heart further hardens. The police catch him red-handed and bring him back to the Bishop. Facing a life behind bars, Jean Valjean's icy, stone-cold eyes look into the eyes of the Bishop, who opts for forgiveness and compassion rather than bitterness. He explains to the police that he gave the silver to Valjean and says to him to not forget also the candlesticks that he gave him. *"Forget not, never forget that you have promised me to use this silver to become an honest man.... Jean Valjean, my brother: you belong no longer to evil, but to good. It is your soul that I am buying for you. I withdraw it from dark thoughts and from the spirit of perdition, and I give it to God!"* The Bishop not only gives him his freedom, he gives him a new life. By showing him that true love is focused on others rather than the self, he gives him a new purpose. He gives him a heart of flesh.

It's exactly the divine transaction that commenced in a stable in Bethlehem about two thousand years ago. Christ's entrance into the world in human form with a human body and a tiny beating heart allowed us to trade our hearts of stone for hearts of flesh. It's just as Ezekiel explained. *"I will give you a new heart and put a new spirit in you; I will remove from you your heart of stone and give you a heart of flesh. And I will put my Spirit in you and move you to follow my decrees and be careful to keep my laws."* The incarnation of God in human form enables us to love, to know how to love. Without the example of God's love, without the love of Christ made flesh among us, we can't love. We don't know how. Without Christmas, we'd be living the futile lives of trying to love with hearts of stone. It just doesn't work. As the Apostle John explains, *"This is how we know what love is: Jesus Christ laid down his life for us. And we ought to lay down our lives for our brothers and sisters."*

And what of Jean Valjean? What becomes of him? Being given a heart of flesh and being given the example of sacrificial love, he undergoes a spiritual heart transplant and begins to live for others, profoundly impacting many others for good. It sounds a bit like the prescription for our lives, except that the ultimate gift of God coming into the world is a bit more priceless than a pair of candlesticks.

## Let's Talk About It:

-What does today's painting show us about the Scripture passage?

-Why do we need God to give us a heart of flesh?

-How do you need to alter the course of your life to more fully live for others?

## Prayer:

*Father, thank you for sending your son into this world, that we might know what true love really is and that we might truly love others with our hearts of flesh. In His Name, Amen.*

43

We love to play the scriptwriter. Give us a pen and a few reams of paper, and we'll gladly script out the plot of our lives. We'll paint the story of our lives in glowing colors, allowing just enough heartache to make the tale interesting, but including copious twists of fortune and goodwill to make the chronicle enjoyable. Who wants to endure the struggle of fate for more than a few pages anyway? Let us love deeply, live the American Dream, dance in time to the music and ride off into the sunset at a ripe old age. And since we're the ones penning this saga, why not just channel Enoch or Elijah and close the book with a dramatic chariot ride into the pearly gates. Amen. End of story.

While we clutch Control like it's a lifeline, ultimately we're merely actors in the grand drama that the Author of Salvation is writing on the pages of our lives. As we look back on the past 2,000 pages or years of history, it's a story that only the Father could write, one that simply sparkles with the Master's artistic touch. One place we see this is in the prophecy of Micah 5.

At first glance we totally get it. We're all too familiar with this story. In the midst of an enslaved and oppressed people, a small-town boy rises out of obscurity to battle the odds, ascend to prominence and make his way to the throne where he rules with more authority than Nebuchadnezzar. With a military force more populated than some world capitals, he overthrows all foes, institutes a peaceful regime and reigns in power for the rest of his days. The credits roll at film's end, and we applaud, having witnessed a true rags-to-riches success story.

The thing is, God's story doesn't follow the same formula. His story always turns the ways of the world upside down. His story always flips our orientation heavenward. Yes, Micah's prophecy still details the people who've been *"abandoned"* and describes how the Messiah will reign and how *"his greatness will reach to the ends of the earth."* Notice though the key difference between the way our Hollywood, *Braveheart*-inclined minds think and the way God operates. *"And he will be our peace."* In God's world, power doesn't pave the way for peace. Military might isn't the precursor for calm. In God's story, *He* is the peace. *Jesus* brings the peace that seems so elusive in this world. It's a peace evident not in the lack of skirmishes or gladiator-like battles, but in the stillness of our souls. When the Prince of Peace comes, we will know and live true peace. We won't need to grasp for power or control because we'll have the Messiah who is our peace. This is the true promise of Christmas, that Immanuel- "God with us"- means peace on earth.

Oh, and one more thing. Just to further encourage us to relinquish the quills and let God be the storyteller, look at the little town of Bethlehem. The name means "house of bread." A mere mortal couldn't have scripted the story any better. What better place could there be for the "Bread of Life" to be born?

## Let's Talk About It:

-What does today's painting show us about the Scripture passage?

-In what ways have you wanted to script your life instead of allowing God to tell His story through you?

-Share about the areas of your life where you need the power of his peace.

## Prayer:

*Dear Father, not only have you promised us peace on earth, but you sent your own son to be our peace, our Prince of Peace. Thank you, Father. Amen.*

The church I belong to recently adopted a new mission statement: "God in Christ. Christ in Us. Us in the world." Taken by itself, the third part of my church's mission statement seems daunting: *"Us in the world."* This world's embrace is often as welcoming as a porcupine's. *Trial. Despair. Heartache. Stress.* These are the descriptors of *"Us in the world."* Relationships strained. Energy drained. We often feel singed by the sting of sin. Watching the nightly news is an exercise in wide-eyed, sobering resignation, the telecast filled with heinous crimes and perilous times. Even the days that dawn with new promise and a renewed commitment to doing good seem to get scorched by the ways of a world beyond our control. In short, *"Us in the world"* is to step into the fire with both feet. Trying to make sense of a world that burns us in more ways than one causes us to repeatedly utter the cry of *"Why?"* *"Why, Lord, is life so hard?"* *"Why, Lord, do we face persecution?"* *"Why, Lord, do good things happen to bad people?"*

Shadrach, Meshach and Abednego

were well-acquainted with our plight and maybe even the nagging question of "why?" though there's no hint of it in Daniel 3. Determined to "do good" and continue to worship the one true God, their obedience gets rewarded with a visit to the incinerator. Tied and clad with robes, trousers and turbans, they get tossed in the fire. Certain martyrdom looms unless God rescues them. Little did they know that a Christmas story was about to break out in the middle of the fire.

The angel of the Lord appears and neither douses the flames nor removes the trio from the inferno. Instead, he joins them in the midst of the fire. He enters their world and keeps them safe. Essentially the world gets an extended, engaging trailer for the real Christmas story about 600 years before its release. When His people face a fire-filled world, God simply steps into the world with them.

*"Us in the world"* isn't quite the harrowing plight when we look at the context and see the three words preceding it. *"Christ in us."* Facing the fires of a harsh world becomes much easier when we realize what Christmas really is. The Incarnation seems like a fancy way of saying that Christ took on flesh, but essentially it means that Jesus stepped into the fire with us. We still might wonder about the weighty question of *"Why?"* but when we realize that Christ is standing in the fire with us, we understand. We might yearn for deliverance from the fires of our lives, but the fact that Christ joins us in the fray and in the pain of our lives keeps us from really getting harmed.

Maybe the next time we see a candle burning at Christmas we can remember not only the Light of the World, but the fact that that Light stepped into the fire with us. *"God in Christ, Christ in Us, Us in the World."* Maybe "motivating" rather than "daunting" is the best word to use to describe it.

---

## Let's Talk About It:

-What does today's painting show us about the Scripture passage?

-In what ways have you experienced the *"fires"* of this world?

-Share about a time in which you felt Jesus stepping into the fire with you and sustaining you.

---

## Prayer:

*Jesus, your coming into this world is the greatest blessing we could ever know. Thank you for loving us enough to enter our sorrows and carry us through. In your Name, Amen.*

Any good story that's worth its weight in parchment has at its core a gripping conflict that hooks the reader and carries him or her along like a willing trout through hundreds of pages of water until it gets all the way reeled in at the climax of the story. Throughout the tale the author unrolls the plot in such a way that the twists and turns of the story either subtly or overtly point the reader towards the highest point of action in the story when the protagonist dramatically solves the conflict.

The Bible's no exception to this formula. Ultimately the Word of God is the story of a people enslaved in sin and a loving Father who rescues them from their desperate fate by thrusting his own beloved son into their world to bring them salvation by giving his life for theirs. Thus, the Bible as a story, as the greatest story ever told, sometimes shouts it and sometimes whispers it, but throughout the book, it foreshadows the coming of the

Messiah. The aroma of Jesus wafts through the Word.

Such is the case with the book of Ezra. Feeling convicted and wanting to restore the symbol of God's presence within his people, Ezra and crew begin the process of rebuilding the temple. They know that God's house needs to be in order; the place where He dwells needs to be worthy of his presence. In an effort that would put Extreme Makeover Home Edition to shame, Ezra and the rest of the returned exiles lay the foundation for the temple. Their endeavor evokes both joy and sorrow from the masses who witness the rebuilding. And, like so much of the Holy Word, it points to Jesus and to another restoration project, the one that commenced with the Son of God's entrance into this world.

No, Jesus never used his carpenter skills to rebuild the temple in Jerusalem. He did though devote his life to the greatest restoration project the world has ever known, restoring his people to himself. In doing so, Jesus established a new temple, a new dwelling place. No longer would God dwell in the Holy of Holies, but rather in the hearts of his people. It's significant that three places where Jesus stayed- a manager, a cross and a tomb- were all left empty by Christ. It's because he lives now in his new Church which is his body, the people of God.

It's something to contemplate as we preen in front of a mirror in a mad rush to get to church on time. Jesus continually takes what we know and turns it upside down. We tend to revert back to the mindset of the Israelites, thinking that as we pass through the temple curtain, we're encountering a hallowed place. We might see ourselves as rather ordinary people going to a holy place. In actuality, because of Christmas and the divine restoration project that Jesus orchestrated, we're actually a holy people gathering together in a rather ordinary place.

Maybe that might change the way we look at ourselves in the mirror.

## Let's Talk About It:

- What does today's painting show us about the Scripture passage?
- How does the aroma of Jesus waft through the story of Ezra?
- Why does Jesus no longer dwell only in the temple?

## Prayer:

*Jesus, thank you for loving us so much that you've come to live in us. May we make our lives beautiful and worthy of being called your new temple. In your Name, Amen.*

A Gallup poll of a couple of years ago asked a thousand random Americans a few questions to gauge their attitudes and opinions regarding Christmas. One question asked, "What's the best thing about Christmas?" Over 80% answered "Spending time with family." A predictable, follow-up question mirrored the first. "What's the worst thing about Christmas?" Ninety percent responded, "Spending time with family."

We hear statistics like that and chuckle while at the same time reluctantly nod our heads and realize how true we've found them to be. We know that the annual family Christmas gathering in a few days brings together a sumptuous feast along with the uncle who likes his eggnog a little too much and the extended cousins who make fruitcakes seem nut-less by comparison. As the old adage goes, you can choose your friends, but you can't choose your family . . . unless you're

God.

A look at Christ's family tree in Matthew 1 proves to be an enlightening exercise. Sure, there are the stalwarts, the giants of the faith who take up prominence on the genealogy. Abraham and Jacob and David, the Hebrews 11 Hall-of-Famers, obviously played prominent roles in the line of Christ. But look at the women, God's grandmas if you will, who are listed. Normally the practice of listing women in a genealogy is about as likely as Black Angus catering a vegan convention, but our God delights in the unlikely. The women he includes might be considered to be "undesirables." There's Tamar, who disguised herself as a prostitute for her father-in-law. There's Rahab, the courtesan of Jericho. There's Ruth, a barren widow. And there's Bathsheba, the adulteress who slept with David. In the eyes of the world, undesirable. In God's eyes, they're vessels of grace. Notice that God doesn't just tolerate the unsavory; he uses them in the most important project in the history of the world: the redemption of his people.

Too often we see the EGR (Extra Grace Required) folks in our families and plan to cultivate the virtue of patience. If we can just tolerate Uncle Edmund's political rants for an entire evening, we feel like we've earned a medal. We rest our heads securely on our pillows, satisfied that even though our fingernails nearly drew blood as they dug into our palms in our perpetually clenched fists all night, we never became unglued.

Reading through the line of Christ shows us the need for a new perspective. God doesn't just tolerate the imperfect. He works through them to accomplish his purposes and proclaim his renown to the nations. As 2 Corinthians 12:9 explains, *"My grace is sufficient for you, for my power is made perfect in weakness."*

Maybe as we look around the circle at our family and maybe even more so with the family of God, we can see not just the annoying members who try our patience, but rather see them for who they are- vessels of grace through whom God wants to display his mighty power. Maybe doing so will change the way we look at the birth of Christ, whose own family included a bunch of these folks.

---

## Let's Talk About It:

-What does today's painting show us about the Scripture passage?

- Why would God choose such unsavory characters to be a part of his family?

- How can we be better prepared to embrace and accept our family members this year?

## Prayer:

*Father, help us to see ourselves as we really are- imperfect, broken people who are made new and whole because you've adopted us into your family. In your Name, Amen.*

It's hard to get a full appreciation for the weight of Gabriel's blessed prophecy that gets lofted into Mary's life. A young, teenage virgin, she receives the startling news that she's going to be the mother of God. Imagine the typical flighty middle schooler getting the memo that she's going to deliver a keynote speech at the UN, and you might be nearing the right country, much less the right ballpark. Understandably Mary's troubled and terrified. *"'How will this be,' Mary asked the angel, 'since I am a virgin?'"* Notice though that for Mary, an emerging woman of God, disbelief is only a brief precursor to doxology. At the end of her angelic encounter Mary affirms her role in the grand drama of salvation. *"'I am the Lord's servant,' Mary answered. May your word to me be fulfilled.'"*

Essentially Mary's going through what we might deem a "major deal," a time in life where stress and anxiety and anticipation and hope all converge to consume our thoughts and hearts. A time kind of like a normal Christmas season. Her song that follows is instructive for the proper perspective to possess in the midst of God's working in our lives: praise for the past and promise for the future.

Mary sees the impending first Christmas as the culmination of God's working in the Old Testament. She has a firm grasp of history. Her song mirrors Miriam's song after the deliverance from slavery in Egypt, except that now the deliverance is not from a ruthless people, but rather from sin and that deliverance is going to come in the form of her son. Notice also the plethora of past tense verbs in her song: "performed," "scattered," "filled," and "sent." She praises God for the past, that's He's remembered Israel and remembered his pledge to Abraham to make him the father of many nations. When God's people face the watershed moments in life, the first thing to do is glance in the rearview mirror and give praise for the past.

As Christ-followers though, life isn't just about looking backwards. Mary sees God's promise for the future. *"My soul glorifies the Lord and my spirit rejoices in God my Savior, for he has been mindful of the humble state of his servant. From now on all generations will call me blessed, for the Mighty One has done great things for me—holy is his name."* Notice that Mary offers her *"magnificat"* before Jesus is born, before she feels the baby kicking in her belly, before all of this comes to be. God has simply promised that these things will come to pass. For Mary- for any devoted Christ follower- God's promise for the future is more definite than any scientific law. As Elizabeth noted, *"Blessed is she who has believed that the Lord would fulfill his promises to her."*

Maybe Mary's original Christmas song should be our Christmas song, the melody that our lives play as we approach Christmas morning. We look back and give praise for all the ways in which God has delivered us in the past, and we look forward to the promise that God offers for the future. If it's good enough for the mother of God, then it should be good enough for us too.

## Let's Talk About It:

-What does today's painting show us about the Scripture passage?

-In what ways have you seen God keeping his promises to you in your personal life?

-At Christmas this year, what's your "song"?

## Prayer:

*Father, just as you've led us in the past, so you'll lead us in the future. Thank you for being a God who keeps his word and always promises to deliver his people. We love you. Amen.*

Christmas, more so than any other yearly feast or festival, is a holiday awash in song. On the radio, in the stereo, through the iPod, we lose ourselves in the various carols of the season. In fact, right here, right now, let's take a break from the regularly scheduled devotional and sing. Pick a favorite Christmas tune and belt out a few verses together. . . Yes, go ahead. Singing's good for the soul. No one's stopping you. Chances are if your holiday gathering involves members of the Von Trapp Family Singers sitting around the circle, you're already seven measures deep into a glorious four-part harmony, maybe even with eight different instruments. If, on the other hand, you've got the natural musical ability of a wildebeest, this choral opportunity is decidedly more daunting. At any rate, we can all understand that any proper Christmas season means plenty of song.

Furthermore,                 singing

distinguishes the children of God.In few other places in society do people gather together and sing. Sure, the Memorial Day ceremony might rouse a few choruses of "God Bless America," but by and large, most non-Christian folks don't assemble on a weekly basis and sing publicly. It's a pattern ordained by God. To be a child of God is to sing. In the face of the terrifying coldness and the deafening silence that the world shouts at us, God's people sing.

In the book of Zephaniah God shows his children what will happen after they've experienced the silence of great suffering. *"The Lord your God is with you, the Mighty Warrior who saves. He will take great delight in you, in his love he will no longer rebuke you, but will rejoice over you with singing."* God's singing shatters the silence, filling the void with the wondrous melody of his love for his people.

In Luke 1 Zechariah endures months of silence after the pronouncement of his future son. When his writes the name "John," his tongue loosens and . . . he sings. He sings because God has done great things. He sings because God is faithful. He sings because God has kept his promise. He sings *"because he has come to his people and redeemed them."* He sings because God's plan of rescuing his beloved is now coming to fruition. He sings because in the face of whatever the world throws our way, God's people sing.

But those who don't sing- those who can't fathom the love of an almighty God- often accuse Christians of serving a God who's silent in the face of suffering. They see the bad things happening to good people and wag their finger at God and say, "Huh? Where are you? Why do you let the suffering continue?" What they fail to see is what the birth of Jesus really is. Christmas is a loving God seeing the desperate plight of a world mired in the silence of suffering and sin and gloriously breaking that silence with a song. When you gather together tomorrow morning, what better way to celebrate the Savior's birth than by joining together with the church throughout history, with the heavenly hosts and with God himself and raising the rafters with song.

## Let's Talk About It:

-What does today's painting show us about the Scripture passage?
-What is your favorite Christmas song? Why?
-In what areas of your silence do you need more of God's song?

## Prayer:

*Father, thank you for the beautiful melody that you continue to play in the song of our lives. Thank you for your Son and for the music He is to our souls. Amen.*

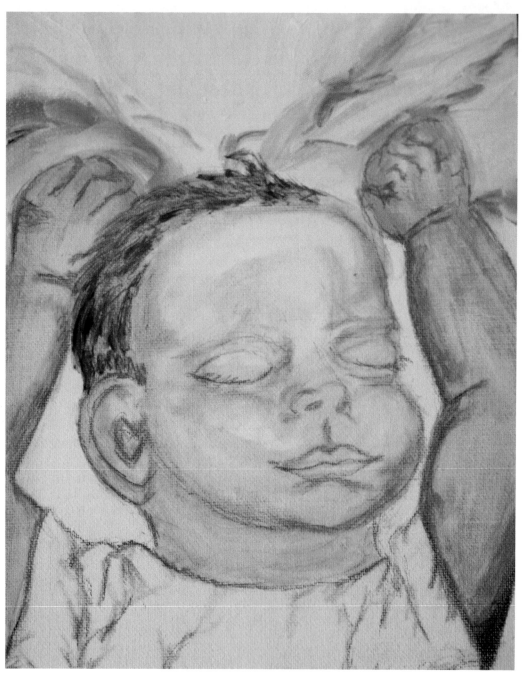

Anyone who's ever been in a family with a baby surely understands the true nature of Christmas. Soon after conception, the family calendar morphs into one that revolves around a 40-week time period. Life is measured according to how many of the magical 40 weeks are left. As the due date draws near, the chronometer switches to a daily ticker, with Mom and Dad knowing exactly the number of days until the baby's supposed to come. Throughout the process a prickling sense of anticipation peppers the emotions as a family "gets ready" for the blessed event to occur.

It's the same with Christmas. No other holiday provokes such sense of anticipation.    Stores chart the number of shopping days left.    Kids finger presents, shaking and making like amateur fortune tellers, trying to glean through osmosis the contents of the wrapped boxes of magic.    Moms frantically bake a delectable smorgasbord of mouthwatering treats.    Dads maniacally finish end-of-the-year projects, trying to put the wrap on all fiscal matters.    Even as a church we gradually illuminate the Advent wreath, the lit candles a symbol of the divine countdown shared by all of society.

It's the same countdown that's been shared throughout history, ever since that first dubious bite of fruit. Ever since the shackles of sin clamped around the human race's ankle, mankind has wallowed in darkness, waiting for a light, waiting for that center candle- the Christ candle- to be lit.    Groaning in the strain of sin and desperately anticipating the rescue, the one that comes in the form of the Savior of the world.    Consider a couple thousand years of pent-up longing for deliverance and you might see the necessity of a hundred thousand angels lighting up the sky to shout the birth of the Messiah, the great deliverer of his people.

Christmas is surely a time for celebration.    God is with us. Jesus is born.    The rescue plan is complete. Sound the trumpets.    Raise your voices.    Throw hands in the air.    Hug each other.    Clap hands.    Lift high the name of Jesus.    Celebrate fiercely and unashamedly.

And realize that, ironically, this season that's all about anticipation, is celebrated best with even more, greater . . . anticipation.    God has kept his promise.    He's given his Son.    Jesus has come and as we celebrate his coming, we look forward to his coming again.    As followers of the Christ-child, we best celebrate this day by looking ahead to the day that will be unlike any other day.    We long for the day when as the song *Days of Elijah* says, "He comes, riding on the clouds, shining like the sun, at the trumpet call." As we celebrate God with us, we eagerly await when *"He will wipe every tear from their eyes.    There will be no more death or mourning or crying or pain, for the old order of things has passed away."*

As we close this devotional and this season, we add our voice to the holy call at the end of Revelation and shout, *"Amen. Come, Lord Jesus."*

## Let's Talk About It:

-What does today's painting show us about the Scripture passage?
-What is the best part of celebrating Christmas?
-What do you long for as a follower of the Christ-child?

## Prayer:

*Holy Father, we praise you for sending your son to us. May we celebrate with open arms and open hearts the wondrous love that you have for us. In the Name of the Messiah, Amen.*

# About Us

Blake A. Hiemstra is the author of *The Year of Living Metaphorically: Ramblings and Reflections on Life, Faith, Family and the Creatures Known as Middle Schoolers.* He also blogs at *The Write Project* (www.writeproject.wordpress.com) where he "looks for light in a weary world." He swims the treacherous middle school waters every day as a teacher and loves every minute of it. He lives in Visalia, California, with his beloved wife Carla and four passionate little tykes: Jacie, Kenna, Avery and Carter. He dreams of one day penning the next Great American Novel and managing to keep his desk clean for more than 24 consecutive hours.

Andrea Van Wyk Kamper is an artist, educator, and the kids director at her church. Andrea has been creating art since she was 5, graduating with her B.A. in elementary education and art/fine art from Dordt College, and a Masters degree in theology, specializing in Christian counseling. Andrea is passionate about the topic of integrating art and Christianity, thus completing her thesis *The Approaches of Art in a Child's Faith Formation.* Andrea's past experiences of teaching in the classroom, working with inner city kids, as well as missions trips weave together to engage kids in a relationship with Jesus through art. Andrea enjoys the adventure of parenting with her husband Myron and their sons Jacob and Myer.

# Sources

**Foreword**
 "*These things are written*": John 20:31
 "*Lots of stories*": Sally Lloyd-Jones, *The Jesus Storybook Bible* (Grand Rapids: Zonderkidz, 2007)

**Introduction**
 "*A shoot will come up*": Isaiah 11:1
 "*Became flesh and made*": John 1:14

**Day 1**
 "*God saw*": Genesis 1:31

**Day 3**
 "*God saw how corrupt*": Genesis 6:12
 "*Floodgates of the heavens*": Genesis 7:11

**Day 4**
 "*For all have*": Romans 3:23

**Day 5**
 "*Is able to do*": Ephesians 3:20
 "*So he left*": Genesis 12:4

**Day 6**
 "*And when I think*": Stuart K. Hine, "How Great Thou Art",1949

**Day 7**
 "*You intended to harm*": Genesis 50:20
 "*Father, forgive them*": Luke 23:34

**Day 8**
 "*Born a child*": Charles Wesley, "Come Thou Long-Expected Jesus", 1744

**Day 9**
 "*It would have been*": Exodus 14:12
 "*But I will gain glory*": Exodus 14:4
 "*I am the Way*": John 14:6

**Day 11**
 "*Do not consider*": I Samuel 16:7
 "*A man after*": Acts 13:22
 "*All a man's ways*": Proverbs 21:2
 "*He had no beauty*": Isaiah 53:2

**Day 12**
 "*As surely as*": II Kings 5:16
 "*Come, all you*": Isaiah 55:1

**Day 13**

*"Yea, Lord we greet"*: John F. Wade, "O Come, All Ye Faithful", 1743
*"Did what was right"*: II Kings 22:2
*"Come thou long-expected"*: Westly

**Day 14**

*"Lays down his life"*: John 10:11

**Day 15**

*"From that time on"*: Isaiah 9:7

**Day 16**

*"I have come home"*: C.S. Lewis, *The Last Battle* (New York: Macmillan, 1956)

**Day 17**

*"Despised and rejected"*: Isaiah 53:3-6

**Day 18**

*"Forget not, never forget"*: Victor Hugo, *Les Miserables* (New York: Modern Library, 1992)
*"I will give you a new heart"*: Ezekiel 36:26-27
*"This is how we know"*: I John 3:16

**Day 19**

*"His greatness will reach"*: Micah 5:4-5

**Day 22**

*"My grace is sufficient"*: II Corinthians 12:9

**Day 23**

*"How will this be"*: Luke 1:34-45
*"I am the Lord's servant"*: Luke 1: 38
*"My soul glorifies the Lord"*: Luke 1:46-48
*"Blessed is she who"*: Luke 1:45

**Day 24**

*"The Lord your God"*: Zephaniah 3:17
*"Because he has come"*: Luke 1:68

**Day 25**

*"He comes, riding"*: Robin Mark, "Days of Elijah" (Integrity Music, 1996)
*"He will wipe away"*: Revelation 21:4
*"Amen. Come, Lord Jesus"*: Revelation 22:20

14225419R00034

Made in the USA
Charleston, SC
28 August 2012